EVERYDAY MINDFUL MANTRAS FOR MINIS

Written by

ERIN MARRAZZO

Illustrated by

EMILY HERCOCK

Everyday Mindful Mantras for Minis
Copyright © 2023 by Erin Marrazzo

Paperback ISBN: 979-8-9891787-1-1

Library of Congress Control Number: 2023918896

First printing edition 2023

Written by Erin Marrazzo
Illustrated by Emily Hercock

I dedicate this book to my inspirations for writing it: the elementary school students I have taught over the past twenty years, my children, Jonathan and Victoria, and my inner child who would have benefited from having these mantras when I was younger.

Why Everyday Mindful Mantras for Minis?

The words we tell ourselves matter. Our thoughts shape what we believe about ourselves and the world around us. This is especially true for children, who are still learning how to be in the world.

In this busy, quick-paced world that we live in, there is always somewhere to go and something to do, with little downtime. In recent years, children have become more isolated and withdrawn due to many factors, including excessive use of technology and the Covid-19 pandemic. Children's mental health, self-confidence, and social skills have all suffered as a result. Many children are struggling with big feelings like anxiety, fear, and anger.

It is crucial to teach kids tools to be more mindful and help them regulate their emotions. Mantras are a powerful mindfulness tool for children. This book gives children the mantras they need to believe in themselves and cope with the challenges they face in their lives. Using these mantras can empower kids to shape their own emotional health and create a positive future. If children repeat these mantras often, the words will become their reality.

BENEFITS
of a Regular Mindfulness Practice for Children

Children who regularly practice mindfulness:

- Show improved focus and academic performance.

- Gain discipline and self-control.

- Show an increase in self-confidence and self-awareness.

- Become mindful and learn how to keep calm.

- Learn how to remain in the present without worrying about the past or the future.

- Learn how to use their breathing to reduce stress and anxiety.

- Are better able to regulate their emotions.

- Are better able to cope with life changes and difficult situations.

THE 3 M'S
for Parents, Educators, and Caregivers

What Are Mantras?

Mantra is an ancient Sanskrit term derived from "*man*" meaning "*mind*" and "*tra*" meaning "*release.*" Mantras are words or phrases that we can repeat to make us feel good or use as mind tools to motivate us to be our best selves.

What Does It Mean to be Mindful?

Being mindful means being in the present moment and fully paying attention to what is happening right now without judgment.

What is Meditation?

Meditation is a practice of concentration, and the goal is to bring yourself back to the present moment as often as you need to.

THE 3 M'S
for Minis

Mantras

Mantras are a group of words we tell ourselves, again and again, to help us feel better or to help us feel good about ourselves.

Mindfulness

Mindfulness means paying attention to what you are doing. It means slowing down and noticing your breathing, how you feel, and what is happening right now.

Meditation

Meditation is an activity that helps us to concentrate and focus. Whenever we are doing something mindfully, we are practicing meditation.

HOW DO I MEDITATE?

1. Find a quiet and comfortable place.

2. Sit with your legs crossed or in any way that feels comfortable for you.

3. Rest your hands on your lap.

4. Close your eyes if it feels safe, or if you would like, keep them open.

5. Take a deep breath in through your nose and slowly let it out through your mouth.

   - As you inhale, pretend to smell some sweet, fragrant flowers.

   - As you exhale, pretend you are trying to gently blow out some colorful birthday cake candles.

6. Keep practicing.

HOW TO USE
Everyday Mindful Mantras for Minis

Pick an area you would like to improve on, focus on, or want to think more about. Find that mantra topic and choose a few to read, learn, and repeat.

You can silently repeat your mantra during meditation or wherever you are.

You can mindfully write or draw your mantra.

You can record the mantra and listen to it over and over.

You can have someone say the mantra and then repeat it back to them.

Whichever way you choose, be sure to bring these mantras into your everyday life in some way!

Mantras That Help Us Grow

Mantras to Help with Situations

MANTRAS THAT HELP US GROW

It's nice to feel proud of ourselves as we grow.

You have done so much right; I thought you should know.

PROUD Like a Sunflower

I am like a sunflower.

I stand tall and strong.

I am PROUD of who I am.

I keep my face towards the sun and grow.

I choose to see the BEST in myself.

Lions are known to be big and strong.
Be brave like a lion, and roar out your song.

BRAVE Like a Lion

I am like a lion.

I am BRAVE.
I am STRONG.
I am COURAGEOUS.

I hold my head up
high and speak
boldly.

I have POWER
within me.

It feels good to be included, and there's space for us all.
So, ask someone to join you; go give them a call.

BELONGING Like a Rainbow

I am like a rainbow.

I am **BRIGHT.**
I am **COLORFUL.**
I am **BEAUTIFUL.**

I am kind
to all.

I am accepted for who I am.
I **LIKE** who I am.

I belong.

Butterflies change to become something new.
They are free to fly, and you can be, too!

FREE Like a Butterfly

I am like a butterfly.

I am free to fly.

I can spread
my wings.

I am light
and free.

I am open to change.

I go through changes
to become something
BEAUTIFUL.

Every star is unique, sparkly, and bright.
You are like a star shining your light.

I am like a star.

I am bright.

I am SPECIAL and UNIQUE.

I shine for others to see.

I light up the world
by being MYSELF.

Being on a team is so much fun.
Put your brains together and get things done.

Showing TEAMWORK

I work well with others.

I am a team player.

I share ideas and listen to others' ideas.

I am fair, and I do my share.

I take turns with others.

Being responsible is doing what you said you would do.
Finish your homework, and complete your chores, too.

Being RESPONSIBLE

First, I get the job done, and then I can have fun.

I don't blame others.

I am responsible for me.

Others can count on me.

Being loving and kind is a beautiful thing.
Bringing joy to others can make your heart sing.

Being LOVING and KIND

I am kind, caring, and loving.

I spread joy.

I have a big heart.

Making someone's heart happy makes mine happy, too.

I cheer people up when I can.

I breathe in love, and I breathe out kindness.

Peace is that soothing feeling you get,
When everything feels right, calm, and set.

Feeling at PEACE

I am peaceful.

I breathe in peace.

All is well
at this moment.

I bring peace
to others.

Peace begins
with ME.

Telling the truth from the start is smart.
Being honest will make you feel calm in your heart.

HONESTY

I am honest with myself and others.

I admit when I am wrong.

I feel free when I tell the truth.

I know telling the truth hurts less than a lie.

Integrity means standing up for what is right,
while being yourself; bold, brave, and bright.

I say what I
believe.

I **keep** my **promises**.

I am
trustworthy.

I do **what is right**
even when no one
else is looking.

Having manners means saying please and thank you,
and waiting your turn.
Manners matter to others, as you will soon learn.

MANNERS

I say **please**
when I ask.

I say **thank you**
when I receive
something.

I say I'm **sorry**
when I'm wrong.

I wait my
turn **calmly**.

I **greet** people
with a hello.

I say goodbye
kindly.

I **ask permission**
when I need to.

Self-awareness means knowing what you say, think, or do,
May have consequences that affect others, too.

SELF-AWARENESS

I **pause** and **think** before I speak.

I **stop** and **think** before I do.

I speak **kindly** and **respectfully.**

I show my **best** self to others.

I don't know everything, but I am **proud** of what I do know.

Being grateful means appreciating what you have every day.
It helps us feel happy whatever life brings our way.

GRATITUDE

I am **thankful** for the people in my life.

I am **grateful** that I am alive and healthy.

I get to use my strong body and mind.

I am **grateful** for small things; I am grateful for **ALL** things.

I have a **loving** heart.

Being confident means you feel sure and prepared.
You can try new things without feeling scared.

SELF-CONFIDENCE

I am ready and prepared.

There are things that I can do well.

I can do this.

I believe in me.

I already have everything I need for success within me.

When you feel creative, ideas come to your mind.
You might paint a picture or come up with a rhyme.

CREATIVITY

I am creative.

I have great ideas that are all my own.

I have a big imagination.

I am a creative thinker.

I come up with smart ideas.

To persevere means to keep on going.
You never stop trying
and keep your effort flowing.

PERSEVERANCE

I won't give up.

I keep going so I
keep on growing.

Great things take time
to accomplish.

Things that
grow take time
to show.

I stick with it
when I feel like
quitting.

Respect is a feeling we all deserve and seek.
Treat others with kindness in what you do
and how you speak.

RESPECT

I respect myself.
I respect others.

I take care of myself
and my belongings.

I am careful with
other people and their
belongings.

I earn respect from
others by acting
respectfully.

I deserve respect.

You were uniquely made: one of a kind, a special "you."
Please remember this in all you do.

SELF-WORTH

Who I am is enough.

I matter.

I am beautiful.

I am unique.

I was made perfectly.

I don't compare myself to others.

I decide who I am.

I love who I am.

Letting go means knowing what's in your power and what's not.

You can only control yourself, and that is a lot.

I can only control my own thoughts, words, and actions.

I focus on what I can do, not what I can't do.

I cannot control other people.

I let go of hard feelings.

Focusing on yourself means you're in charge of you.
You look inside yourself and see the things you do.

Focus on YOURSELF

I keep the focus on myself.

I don't focus on what others are doing.

I am on my own path.

I am proud of my own decisions.

It isn't easy to forgive and forget,

But it's freeing to give and even better to get!

FORGIVENESS
of Self and Others

I can forgive.

I make mistakes
so I can let others
make mistakes.

I am not bad
if I make a bad choice.

I deserve another chance,
as long as I don't make the
same wrong choice again.

EVERYONE deserves
another chance!

Treat your friends with kindness and hold them dear.
When you need them, true friends will be near.

Being a FRIEND

I am a good friend.

I **listen** to and **respect** my friends.

I cheer on others with **kindness.**

I am **happy** for others.

People want to be around me.

Waiting can feel like a hard thing to do.
Taking deep breaths can make it easier for you.

PATIENCE

I am patient.   I know my turn will come.

Sometimes I need to wait.

Waiting makes me stronger.

Being positive means thinking the best,
Even when hard things put you to the test.

POSITIVE THINKING

I look at the **bright side.**

I am **positive.**

I am **hopeful.**

Good things are on their way.

I **fill my mind** with positive thoughts, even during tough times.

You can make a change by doing your part.
Helping and donating is a good way to start.

Making a DIFFERENCE

I can help others.

I can do my part to help change the world.

I can make a difference.

One small act is all it takes.

MANTRAS TO HELP WITH SITUATIONS

You don't need special occasions to feel happy and great. Repeat these mantras every day for a strong mental state.

EVERYDAY Mantra

I am smart.

I am important.

I am kind.

I am strong.

I can do hard things.

A new school year has so much potential each day.
Think of everything you'll learn as you work and play.

On the FIRST DAYS of SCHOOL

First Day Of SECOND GRADE

First Day Of FOURTH GRADE

I am excited about learning new things.

I am ready for a new school year.

I bring something special to this classroom.

I am going to be successful in my new grade.

I know I belong here.

Tough times may happen to you and to me.
Talking to others helps you face them calmly.

When FACING a DIFFICULT TIME

I am not alone.

I have people who are there for me.

I CAN get through this.

I know tough times WILL pass.

I believe better times are ahead.

Everyone feels nervous at times, it's true.
Getting through these feelings is possible, too.

OVERCOMING NERVOUSNESS

I can do this.

I will do it even though I feel afraid.

I can face my fears.

I don't let fear stop me.

I'm a warrior, not a worrier.

I can tell my worries to go away.

Disappointment in life can be a big blow.
Like losing a game or being told "no."

When DEALING with DISAPPOINTMENT

I tried hard, and things didn't work out, but I'll be okay.

Sometimes what I want is not possible.

People may let me down just like I might let others down.

I won't always get my way, but it's okay.

Feelings may come, and feelings may go.
Dealing with your emotions is important to know.

When Feeling
BIG EMOTIONS

I can feel my feelings.

I share my feelings.

It's okay to have
big feelings.

This feeling will pass.

I know my feelings
aren't facts.

To have anxiety means you feel worried or stressed.
It makes you feel restless, so you can't do your best.

When You Have a Test or SCHOOL ANXIETY

I can do it if I put my mind to it.

I am prepared.

I have a strong mind.

If I do one thing at a time, all will be fine.

I am capable.

DIVISION – 3 DIGITS BY 1 DIGIT SHEET 2
Divide these 2 digit numbers by 2,3,4 or 5.

Being angry is human and not something to hide.
It's okay to feel angry when you're hurting inside.

When Feeling ANGRY

Anger is not the boss of me.

I am in charge, not my anger.

When I breathe in calm, I breathe out anger.

I can feel angry without acting in a way I won't be proud of.

I can walk away, breathe, and respond later.

Calming down means to relax and unwind.
The secret is that it all starts in your mind.

When You NEED CALM

I can take
deep breaths
to relax.

My body is still,
and my mind is quiet.

I breathe in calm
and breathe out worry.

I am calm.

1, 2, 3...
a fully calm me.

Reaching your goals won't happen overnight,
But you can surely achieve them if you use all your might.

When REACHING for GOALS

The more I practice,
the more I improve.

I can achieve
if I believe.

I reach for my goals.

I can't do it yet,
but I will do it.

I follow my
dreams.

I will succeed
because I work
hard.

I am unstoppable.

Some problems feel big, and others seem small.
Believe it's possible for you to solve them all.

When
PROBLEM-SOLVING

I can think for myself.

I make
good choices.

I can problem-solve.

I can trust my
own judgment.

All my problems
can be solved.

I can figure out
what to do next.

My mind is strong,
and I can think this through.

Sleep gives your brain a chance to rest.
It helps your body be at its best.

When it is TIME to REST

I am ready to relax.

I am happy about
the good things
that happened today.

I can let my mind rest.

Sleep is good for me.

I deserve
to rest.

I will have
sweet dreams.

I am ready
to be still.

Mornings are hopeful, refreshing, and new.
It's a brand-new day to be your best "you."

In The MORNING

I am rested and full of energy.

I can take on this day.

I am ready to go.

Today is a fresh start.

I will have a good day no matter what.

I will do great things today.

When MAKING an EFFORT

Good is okay, but better is best.

So always try hard and put yourself to the test.

I give it my all, or I don't do it at all.

I give my best in everything I do.

My best will look different from day to day, and that is okay.

Done well does not have to mean done perfectly.

If I tried my best, I have succeeded.

Sometimes things may happen that you hadn't planned for.
Change may be hard, but you can face it for sure.

When THINGS CHANGE

Change can
sometimes be tough,
but so am I.

I will figure this out.

All will be okay.

I will get used
to this.

To be focused means being here and now.
To stay in the moment, some way, somehow.

When You Must FOCUS

I am ready to learn.

I focus on my work.

I do one thing
at a time.

I keep my eyes
on my goal.

Mistakes can make you braver, stronger, and smarter.
You can use them to grow and get so much farther.

When
MAKING MISTAKES

If I fall, I get back up.

I am human,
and humans
make mistakes.

I don't know everything,
and that's okay.

I haven't figured it
out yet.

I will keep trying.

Making a mistake
means I'm trying.

A mistake is a chance
to start over.

Starting over means moving on from the past.
Let go of things from today, from this week, or last.

When You Have to
BEGIN AGAIN

I won't let one bad event or decision ruin my whole day.

I can begin again now.

I can make things new.

I can turn my day around.

CLOSING MESSAGE

You have the power to change your thoughts and be the best you that you can be.

These mantras can be used anywhere, at any time. You can use them on a walk, on the school bus, in bed before you go to sleep, on the soccer field, or even while you're brushing your teeth. Use them each day, even when things are okay, so you'll remember them when you're having a tough time or need reminders to believe in yourself.

Just remember to keep repeating and keep believing.

ABOUT THE AUTHOR

Erin Marrazzo is an elementary school teacher with over 20 years of experience and a mom of two young children. She has practiced yoga for 15 years and is a certified Children's Yoga and Mindfulness Instructor, registered as RYT 500 and RCYT with Yoga Alliance.

Erin uses affirmations and mantras in her own life to overcome struggles and deal with stress, change, and grief. Erin feels that motivational mantras have helped her mentally, emotionally, and spiritually.

Erin noticed astounding results when she began using these mantras, mindfulness, and yoga in her classroom and in the mindfulness club she facilitates at the school where she teaches. Students began to use her strategies and mantras and found that these tools also helped them to cope. Erin was inspired to write this book to share her ideas and inspiration with others.

Erin wishes she had these tools to help her navigate her own mind when she was younger. As a child, Erin struggled with self-esteem. She never felt good enough, smart enough, or capable enough. When Erin discovered that she could use the power of mantras to change her thoughts, she gained self-confidence.

Erin believes that good mental health is a crucial element to a child's success in all areas of life; she is driven to help boost children's self-confidence wherever she can. Erin hopes that this book will make a positive contribution to children's mental health everywhere.

ABOUT THE ILLUSTRATOR

Emily Hercock has worked as a freelance illustrator for nearly ten years, building her business from the ground up.

As a child, Emily could always be found with a pen and paper in her hand, drawing away at her latest artwork creation.

Emily never believed that she could make a career out of her hobby. But, with a lot of determination and hard work, she has been able to successfully turn her love of art into her own business.

Emily lives in the small, sleepy village of Watlington in the UK, where she resides with her husband, Michael, and thoroughly-mad cats, Missy and Rupert.

ACKNOWLEDGEMENTS

Writing a book is one thing, but developing a manuscript into a published piece for the world to see is no easy feat. I could not have done it without the love and care of some important people in my life.

I'd like to thank *my husband and family* for their unwavering support and encouragement throughout this process. They believed in me and were patiently there for me every step of the way.

A special thanks goes to **Michael Hercock** for his knowledge and talent, and for all the time, effort, and dedication he took in designing and formatting this book. His patience and ability to create my vision was greatly appreciated.

My illustrator, **Emily Hercock**, deserves tremendous recognition for bringing my idea for every mantra topic to life in such a beautiful way. Her talent, patience, and kindness is second to none.

Betty Larrea, my book duola and mentor, deserves great acknowledgement for sharing her invaluable publishing experience and expertise. Working with Betty was essential, and I was blessed to have found her when I did.

Bright Sunflower

YOGA FOR KIDS

LET'S STAY CONNECTED

 @brightsunfloweryogaforkids

www.brightsunfloweryogaforkids.com